GRASPING YOUR ASSIGNMENT

THERE IS GRACE FOR YOUR PLACE

DR. DAVID COPELAND

ENDORSEMENTS

Thank you for allowing me the privilege of having a "first look" at your book!! I'm honored that you thought of me. What a transparent and insightful journey packed with wisdom for those in the pews as well as new and seasoned ministers in every season of our journeys. Thank you for being obedient and taking the time to give of yourself to others. What a wonderful gift and friend you and Pam are to Greg and I!

Pastor Deborah Prihoda
   The Embassy Church
   Rosenberg, Texas

I enjoyed reading the book, "Grasping your Assignment." This is an excellent book for those who want to understand in a greater way what God has called them to. Matthew 22:14 says: "Many are called but few are chosen." Between the calling and the choosing there is a process that God allows one to walk through. This book will help you to locate where you are, and to recognize the process God is taking you through to get there. The life illustrations in this book help with understanding that process. The information in this book will help you in understanding the seasons of transition that God is taking you through to promote you to the place of your assignment. Being faithful in the season of small things is very important. The author shows you the role that faithfulness plays in our life and the importance of having the right kinds of leaders.

Pastor Brad Morgan
New Life Beginnings Church
Pattison, Texas

Understanding what God has called you to and why He has called you is vital — not just for those in vocational ministry — for all believers. In this book, David helps us understand how grace is the key component of our calling and helps us lead a life of legacy through our inheritance and our assignments.

Pastor David Russell
Church of the Highlands
Online Campus Pastor

FOREWORD

What a great honor to write the forward for my friend and Pastor David Copeland. I first met David in the spring of 2002. He held a revival meeting for our church. There was an instant kingdom connection in our relationship. Over the past 17 years, he has preached many times in my church and has always had a word in season.

David has the ability to operate in the spirit of Barnabas. He is an encourager and sees potential in people they cannot see. Mark 3:16 says: Simon to whom he gave the name Peter. One meaning of Simon is a reed blowing here and there. Jesus called Peter a rock. I have seen David do the same thing in my life and others. God has graced him with the gift of mercy to walk with a person until they became what he saw and declared.

2nd Corinthians 12:12 says: "Truly the signs of an Apostle were accomplished among you with all perseverance in signs and wonders and mighty deeds."

One of the signs of an Apostle is all perseverance. Over the years I have known David and seen him persevere in many different situations where lesser men would have quit.

I enjoyed reading the book, "Grasping your Assignment." This is an excellent book for those who want to understand in a greater way what God has called them to. Matthew 22:14 says: "Many are called but few are chosen." Between the calling and the choosing there is a process that God allows one to walk through. This book will help you to locate where you are, and to recognize the process God is taking you through to get there. The life illustrations in this book help with understanding that process. The information in this book will help you in understanding the seasons of transition that God is taking you through to promote you to the place of your assignment. Being faithful in the season of small things is very important. The author shows you the role that faithfulness plays in our life and the importance of having the right kinds of leaders.

Over the past 17 years I have seen David in many settings. I can honestly say that David is a man that practices what he preaches. I recommend this book and encourage you to buy this book for yourself and for others who are seeking to find God's best for their life. The best days for David and Pam and his wonderful family are ahead of them.

Much love,
    Pastor Brad Morgan
    New Life Beginnings Church
    Brookshire, Texas

INTRODUCTION

For many years of my life, I struggled with understanding the full dimension of the call of God for my life. It wasn't until I had been in ministry for almost twenty years I began to understand the will of God and the call of God are progressive in nature. God always shows you the end of a thing before the beginning. In other words, it's a process.

I pray this book will bless you and encourage you, and no matter where you are in the process of finding and fulfilling the will of God, you will be inspired to finish and finish strong.

-Dr. David Copeland
   Revival Now Ministries

CHAPTER ONE

UNDERSTANDING THE DIFFERENCE BETWEEN INHERITANCE AND ASSIGNMENT

There is a general call of God that all of us will carry on our lives until the day we die. You may not be called to preach, to be a missionary or serve as a board member of your local church. But there IS a general call for every believer.

The general call on our lives begins with loving the Lord Jesus with all our hearts and then loving our neighbors as ourselves. Out of that intimacy with Jesus there will come a deeper or a specific call: the call to some type of service for the Lord. It can either be as a layperson in leadership, a bi-vocational minister or full-time ministry. It can be to an auxiliary ministry such as women, youth or music; or God may call you to the ministry of helps. My purpose is not to go into detail on every type of ministry gift; that will be for another time. Some may be reading this book because you are searching for direction in finding God's perfect will for your life. Then you may be reading this book, already knowing the general outline of His calling, but find yourself frustrated with where you are now on your journey.

Him First

Our first step in discerning, knowing and embracing the purpose of God He is calling us to is this: love Him with all our heart, soul, mind, body and strength. Loving and seeking Him first sets the atmosphere to help us understand His direction and calling for any particular day. Then everything about our daily lives (our families, jobs, ministry assignments) will flow from that point of intimacy with our Father. Everything you attempt to do for Jesus without loving Him first is destined for frustration or failure.

Everything we do for God must start from the secret place of prayer. Ten seconds in His Presence can calm all our stress, cement our peace and position us for His plans and purposes for our day, our week, our current season and our overall lives. And out of that place of intimacy we will receive strategies that will work to expand His Kingdom on the earth.

In the early days of my ministry I spent more time being frustrated than fulfilled. I knew I was called to do a work for God but I was frustrated that things were not moving fast enough for "me". Part of the problem was I didn't understand the difference between my inheritance and my assignment. I wish I had a spiritual father in my very earliest days to distinguish this for me.

When we are born again and accept Jesus as Lord of our lives, the Holy Spirit comes to live inside our spirit man. Paul taught us in Ephesians 1:13,14, Holy Spirit is the down payment of our inheritance.

Ephesians 1:13, 14 *[13] In Him you also trusted, after you heard the word of truth, the gospel of your salvation; in whom also, having believed, you were sealed with the Holy Spirit of promise, [14] who[d] is the [e] guarantee of our inheritance until the redemption of the purchased possession, to the praise of His glory. NKJV*

The very moment you commit your life to Jesus Christ, you immediately become a son/daughter of God. You have received the Kingdom of God within you; and the Kingdom has received you. Eternal life is your inheritance. So is healing, provision, protection, power to live for Him, authority to cast out demons and bring Kingdom dominion into your sphere of influence. But look at verse 14 in the Amplified Bible:

Ephesians 1:14 "That [Spirit] is the guarantee of our inheritance [the firstfruits, the pledge and foretaste, the down payment on our heritage], in anticipation of its full redemption and our acquiring [complete] possession of it—to the praise of His glory."

As a Copeland I never received a natural inheritance from my forefathers. There was just nothing left after they died. Except debts and bills and I have enough of those on my own without inheriting theirs.

But as a son of God, Scripture tells me I am a joint heir with Jesus in and with everything Father gave Him as a result of His obedience. Holy Spirit is simply the down payment.

Rom 8:16,17 [16] The Spirit Himself bears witness with our spirit that we are children of God, [17] and if children, then heirs— heirs of God and joint heirs with Christ, if indeed we suffer with Him, that we may also be glorified together.

Inheritance Described

I have been recently reading through the Book of Joshua in my devotional time. It's still amazing to me the detailed tribulations and plagues God unleashed on the Egyptians until Pharaoh finally relented and released the Promised Land children.

In Joshua 5, Moses' successor Joshua, brings the Jews to the possessing of their inheritance: the promised land!

While there are many that deny the Jewish people are the legitimate and rightful owners of the land currently known as Israel, the promise of God to Abraham was his promised seed (which we know comes through Isaac) would possess the entire area from the Euphrates River to the Mediterranean Sea. All the turmoil we are seeing daily in the Middle East is a result of Joshua and the people of that era **not completing the process**. They received their inheritance which was the land, but they didn't complete their assignment which was to drive out the inhabitants of that day. Sadly, because Joshua and the children of Israel failed to drive out the "ites" of the land in that day but chose rather to make a peace treaty with them, we get to live with the ramifications of them not completing their assignment. The land was their inheritance; their assignment was to drive out the Philistines completely.

When we fail to allow the Holy Spirit to convict and convince us of things, attitudes and sinful characteristics of the old nature that need to be removed from our lives, we may know about our inheritance, but our assignments in life will be hindered of total victory because of sin that is ensnaring our lives.

Peter, writing before his death, tells all New Testament believers that the grace and power of the Holy Spirit working in our lives "has given" us all things that pertain to life and godliness. Our inheritance qualifies and empowers us with the necessary tools to live victoriously in every area of our life!

2 Peter 1:2-4 Grace and peace be multiplied to you in the knowledge of God and of Jesus our Lord, ³ as His divine power has given to us all things that pertain to life and godliness, through the knowledge of Him who called us by glory and virtue, ⁴ by which have been given to us exceedingly great and precious promises, that through these you might be partakers of the divine nature, having escaped the [c]corruption that is in the world through lust.

I am very grateful for the grace of God that brought me to salvation. I'm grateful for that grace working in my life. Later in this book I will deal specifically with the grace of God for our assignment, or what I call our measure of grace.

While I am very happy for the new life that the grace message has given people over the last several years, I am afraid many people are misinterpreting the grace message to be a license to sin. I will not labor this, nor am I trying to stir up a theological debate. And I emphatically state here and now that it is His amazing grace that empowers us to walk away from every sin that so easily knocks us out of the race of life. It's His grace that not only liberates us from a religious spirit of works, He also empowers us to gain victory and keep the victory in every area of our lives. This victory will never come by our power of our strength, it has already been purchased with the finished work of Jesus on Calvary's cross.

Hebrews 12:1,2 Therefore we also, since we are surrounded by so great a cloud of witnesses, let us lay aside every weight, and the sin which so easily ensnares us, and let us run with endurance the race that is set before us, ² looking unto Jesus, the author and finisher of our faith, who for the joy that was set before Him endured the cross, despising the shame, and has sat down at the right hand of the throne of God.

My purpose for this writing is to help everyone realize we must mature past only talking about our inheritance and grasp the full understanding that just as grace forgives, gives us life, empowers us to live in victory, that grace also gives us an assignment that only we can complete while we walk this earth. When we settle for only rejoicing in our inheritance and we do not accept our assignment and complete the full process of our assignment, the generations to come will eventually pay a heavy price. Inheritance comes with responsibility. Great inheritance comes with great responsibility.

What is your assignment?

Much has been said in recent years about destiny and purpose for people's individual lives. Sadly, I have to admit, it took me over 25 years of living for God, most of those in full-time ministry for me to understand the difference in my inheritance and my assignment.

Jesus bought us and gave us our inheritance at Calvary. There is absolutely nothing I can do to earn eternal life. It's settled. Faith in His finished work was enough to convince the Father I am now righteous in His sight. All because of the Blood of His Son.

But now that I am a son, I have an assignment. Just as an inheritance comes with responsibility, an assignment always carries responsibility. When you accepted the sacrifice of Jesus Christ for the covering of your sins, you became born again and was put in line for an assignment for the Father. I am not talking about working to earn salvation; but God saves you so you can do something to enlarge and expand His Kingdom during your remaining days on this earth. My assignment carries a grace from God to complete if I am willing to follow His leadership and the prompting of Holy Spirit.

You are the only you that will ever be created! Some call it a gift. Others will call it a talent. Many will simply say you have a unique skill set. It's also a call; a call that comes only from God. It's a calling that carries an anointing. I also call it grace for your place. When the Father created you in your mother's womb you were intricately created to be the only you that will ever be.

Others may sing better... cook differently, analyze

things from a different perspective; but no one will be able to see things the way you see them or understand things from your point of view. This is the uniqueness to which you and every individual on earth is called. Some may achieve greater recognition than you, but you are the only you that will ever be created.

You were created to accomplish things no one else will ever be able to accomplish. Whatever your assignment is will be something that you will enjoy doing. Many people are afraid to submit to the call of God for their lives because they are afraid He will ask them to sell everything they have and move to a far distance country and never see their loved ones ever again.

If you don't hear anything else I say in this book, please listen and hold on to this:

Whatever your assignment is, there will be a grace that accompanies this assignment for you to complete it. God always provides grace for your place. We don't get to choose what gifts we are born with or the unique assignment God calls us to walk in, once He calls us He always gives us a grace to carry out that assignment.

Not everyone is called to preach. Not everyone is called to sing. Very few of us are called to be the CEO's of large corporations. Most of us will never pastor or serve as an elder in a local church. The vast majority of people in the world will never travel outside a 100-mile radius of their home.

But whatever God calls you to do...and wherever God places you, He will give you a desire to be there, a compassion for the people there, and a love for the assignment you will do there.

My Story

I was called to preach at the age of sixteen. Through a dramatic encounter with Jesus, He let me know very clearly

He was calling me to surrender my life and future to Him for full time ministerial service. At that time, I felt for sure He was calling me to preach the Gospel in a pulpit ministry.

The very first message I preached in 1978 at a small rural church in Soddy Daisy, Tennessee, was the absolute worse example for a sermon that has ever been preached. I ministered from Daniel Chapter 3 on Shadrach, Meshach & Abednego. It was the most horrendously awful sermon that had ever been spoken by any preacher of the Gospel since the beginning of time. And it lasted a grand total of three minutes!

When I was finished, the pastor stepped into the pulpit and opened his Bible, looked at me and said, "is that all you have?" He flipped a few pages in his Bible and chatted with the congregation a little then turned to me again and asked, "Are you sure that's all you have?" The whole church laughed. I was devastated! I swore in my heart I would never attempt to preach ever again, as long as I lived. Surely, I misunderstood what God was leading me to do. No one else knew it any better than I did at that moment. Well, everyone else in the place knew it as well. It was so bad, when we arrived at my grandmother's house to drop her off, she reached in her purse and took out $10, reached her hand over the back seat never looking back at me and said, "...son, here's some money, go buy you some books; you're going to need all the help you can get!"

Needless to say, I was crushed! Again and again I swore to God I would never attempt to preach. Ever. Never again. At the time our family had a Gospel singing group that traveled around the Southeastern United States singing in different churches on weekends. During our singing, the anointing would come upon me and I would end up preaching and exhortation more than we would sing. It happened one time in a church in Florida and I went so long in exhorting the people, the pastor finally asked me to stop talking so much and sing so his other group could sing.

While that event crushed me as well, God used it to show me He had indeed called me to a pulpit ministry. After several more years of preaching more than singing, I finally surrendered to the Lord in obedience and committed myself to focus on preaching the Gospel. I still love music. In fact, many times when traveling around the United States, I will have the opportunity to either lead worship or play with some fabulous church musicians prior to speaking in a service. But one thing I do know: I am called to be a preacher of the Gospel! I know for certain I am not the best preacher in the world, but I AM called by my Father God to preach!

There will be a general call of God for the entirety of your life, but at different times, at different seasons and for different reasons, God will change your assignment. This is what I call the specific call of God. Your assignment will take you many places, and maybe into many churches and will ask of you to fill many roles. In 1983 after accepting the fact that my assignment was to preach more than sing, I moved my young family to Lanett, Alabama where I took a job in a local textile mill and accepted the pastorate of a very small church in Valley, Alabama the adjoining town. Our first service at that small church there were six in attendance. My family of four and two other brothers.

My job paid small wages at that time so I was forced to work long hours in a textile mill as well as preach two services on Sunday as well as lead a mid week service on Wednesday night. It also required that I make sure the church building was prepared for the Sunday services as well. In other words, I was also the janitor of the church, the lawn caretaker, and every other "job" that no one else would fill.

One Saturday night about 10pm I remembered the church had not been cleaned. At the time, church attendance had increased to about 7-10 (on a good Sunday), so it naturally fell on me to make sure the sanctuary was ready for the following morning service.

I went to the church to clean and while I was vacuuming the floor and I was praying about the service the next morning, the devil began to whisper in my ear:

"Nobody cares about you or this church."

He continued by saying. "God hasn't called you to preach; if He had, you wouldn't be here vacuuming this floor at almost 11pm on a Saturday night while your wife and children are in bed asleep."

Needless to say, the longer I vacuumed the more I entertained and pondered the words Satan was speaking into my ear. My youth and inexperience coupled with a lack of the Word of God had not yet taught me to cast down imaginations that were contrary to God's Word. As a result, I became very angry. In fact (I'm ashamed to say it) I got so mad, I snatched the electric cord out of the wall and threw (yes, threw) the vacuum cleaner into the closet. With tears rolling down my face, I cried out to God, "this is not fair! My wife and kids are asleep...I haven't seen them all week...I have worked sixty-four hours his week, and here I am, vacuuming the floor at 11pm on a Saturday night!"

Very gently Holy Spirit whispered to my heart, "have you been beaten and hung on a cross to die for people you have never seen? Have you been beaten then pulled outside the city and left to die?"

My tears began to dry up and quietly said, "no".

Holy Spirit whispered and said, "until that happens, shut up and do what I've called you to do!"

Little did I know at that time, this was part of the process of God qualifying me for greater ministry. Part of being called to the ministry is being willing to do whatever it takes to make sure the worship service is of the highest quality it can be. A spirit of excellence should mark everything we ever do for God. Until you are able to clean toilets, cut the grass, pick up paper or straighten chairs (and do it with joy) you will never have the effective pulpit ministry or platform ministry you feel you deserve.

When He whispered those words to me, I gladly went to the closet, pulled out the vacuum cleaner and finished cleaning the carpet. And I actually did it with joy in my heart. And the next morning there was an anointing to preach that I had never experienced before.

What I did not know in 1984 is, that was actually a preparation for the time in which I would have the _opportunity_ to help clean church sanctuaries literally all over the world! He gave me the grace for that place...and used that encounter to teach me...

...the greatest call on a man or woman's life is servanthood.

There will always be grace for your place. But in every assignment, wherever you are in the world (while you ARE a son) you will be placed there to serve.

Ministry is NOT about you; it's about people you come into contact with or are ministering to being able to encounter the transformational Presence of the Living God!

The most frustrating part of finding the fullness of your assignment in life will be the fact that God will give you many tasks before you are allowed to enter into the main assignment He created you for...

Being willing to serve wherever He leads you and being willing to do whatever it takes to add value where you currently are will be a major step in you being able to grasp your assignment.

CHAPTER TWO

BEGINNING TO UNDERSTAND YOUR ASSIGNMENT

The call of God is general in nature...but it will lead to specific assignments. The level you start at should never be the level you remain at for your entire life and service to the Lord. If that is where you are now, you need to repent and recommit to allowing the Holy Spirit to grow you and mature you to a place He can give you more responsibility.

WHILE I TRULY BELIEVE EVERY BELIEVER HAS A CALL OF GOD upon their lives, not everyone is called to be a full-time preacher, pastor or any of the other five-fold ministry gifts. Not everyone is called to be a worship leader. Not everyone is called to preach giant crusade meetings in developing countries in which thousands attend and thousands are saved. Not everyone is called to teach children or young people. One of the greatest travesties we have committed against our children and young people is we birthed programs and then placed people in positions of leadership over these programs who did not have the assignment to be in those positions. Eventually (usually quickly) people burned out, or they "felt called to go to another church" and these positions became revolving doors every three to six months as we were looking for replacements.

NOT EVERYONE IS CALLED TO BE IN FULL TIME CHURCH ministry! Some are called to be doctors, some lawyers. Some are called to be nurses or mechanics...some women are called to be homemakers and powerful mothers to their children and families.

AND SOME ARE SIMPLY CALLED TO BE HELPERS IN A LOCAL church!

I HAVE ALWAYS BEEN A STUDENT OF LEADERSHIP. I HAVE watched and studied different ministers from time to time; their mannerisms, their pulpit delivery, they way the give altar calls, and well as the way the handle people outside the pulpit. I have learned the following:

YOU CAN BE CALLED TO LEADERSHIP...AND NOT BE CALLED TO pastor
    You can be called preach...but not be called to pastor
    You can also be called to pastor...and not be a powerful speaker

.   .   .

Your work will change from time to time as you are faithful to the current assignment that God has given you.

Parable of Talents

In Matthew 25, Jesus spoke a parable that is greatly needed today.

14 "For *the kingdom of heaven is* like a man traveling to a far country, *who* called his own servants and delivered his goods to them. 15 And to one he gave five talents, to another two, and to another one, to each according to his own ability; and immediately he went on a journey. 16 Then he who had received the five talents went and traded with them and made another five talents. 17 And likewise he who *had received* two gained two more as well. 18 But he who had received one went and dug in the ground and hid his lord's money. 19 After a long time the lord of those servants came and settled accounts with them.

20 "So he who had received five talents came and brought five other talents, saying, 'Lord, you delivered to me five talents; look, I have gained five more talents besides them.' 21 His lord said to him, 'Well *done,* good and faithful servant; you were faithful over a few things, I will make you ruler over many things. Enter into the joy of your lord.' 22 He also who had received two talents came and said, 'Lord, you delivered to me two talents; look, I have gained two more talents besides them.' 23 His lord said to him, 'Well *done,* good and faithful servant; you have been faithful over a few things, I will make you ruler over many things. Enter into the joy of your lord.'

²⁴ "Then he who had received the one talent came and said, 'Lord, I knew you to be a hard man, reaping where you have not sown, and gathering where you have not scattered seed. ²⁵ And I was afraid and went and hid your talent in the ground. Look, *there* you have *what is* yours.'

²⁶ "But his lord answered and said to him, 'You wicked and lazy servant, you knew that I reap where I have not sown, and gather where I have not scattered seed.²⁷ So you ought to have deposited my money with the bankers, and at my coming I would have received back my own with interest. ²⁸ So take the talent from him, and give *it* to him who has ten talents.

²⁹ 'For to everyone who has, more will be given, and he will have abundance; but from him who does not have, even what he has will be taken away. ³⁰ And cast the unprofitable servant into the outer darkness. There will be weeping and gnashing of teeth.' NKJV

IN THE STRICTEST RULES OF BIBLICAL INTERPRETATION, THE talent as it is mentioned here is a piece of money. But we can also liken this piece of money to our abilities God gives us at salvation. It is also representative of our calling. How we steward what God gives us reveals our character and positions us for increase and promotion

THE CALLING OF GOD IS JUST THAT: **GOD'S CALLING UPON OUR LIVES!**

While the call of God is general in overall nature, there will be different assignments associated with different seasons in your life.

.   .   .

DURING THE LATE 1980S, MY ASSIGNMENT WAS TO BE A youth pastor. I was obsessed with youth ministry and how to reach students. I studied, lived and breathed youth ministry seven days a week and twenty-four hours a day during that season. And because I was faithful to that assignment and gave my entire focus to it, God blessed it and multiplied our efforts. Thirty years later, there is a residual effect that still comes from that season. Many places we go in the world, Pam and I have a greater influence and connect easier with younger people than we do senior adults. I'm convinced because of the seeds we sowed in that season, God continues to reward us with a special Kingdom connection with students of this generation.

AFTER SEVERAL YEARS OF EFFECTIVE YOUTH MINISTRY, GOD transitioned us into church music ministry. Because I was a musician before I was called to preach, this was an easy fit for me. I was obsessed with Fresh praise and worship music, learning new music, trying to sharpen my skill as a keyboard player. I even wrote several songs and worship chorus' during that season. I also became consumed with learning to understand how to flow in leading a congregation into the Presence of God. Another lesson I learned very quickly was how as a worship leader I was to flow with the pastor during a service. Those lessons during that assignment, I still use to this day!

THE GREATEST LESSON I LEARNED DURING THAT SEASON WAS learning to flow with a pastor in any given service. This one subject has caused much hurt and misunderstandings between worship leaders and Lead Pastors in churches all over the world. Worship leader, no matter where you go, if you are called to be a worship leader, you will always be working under another man's leadership. If your pastor is "quenching the Spirit" in the services, why did you go there to begin with? Did you go there because God called you to serve this man's ministry, or did you go for a check and an opportunity to amaze people with your gift?

WE DESPERATELY NEED PEOPLE WHO WILL ALLOW GOD TO call them to a specific city; then for people to allow God to call them to a specific church; then stay there and bloom for the Kingdom of God's sake!

AFTER SEVERAL YEARS OF BEING FAITHFUL TO THAT assignment, I was asked to be the Lead Pastor at the church we served at for almost fifteen years. I was consumed with growing as a leader of a flock, touching the flock, being touchable by the flock...ministering to their needs and seeing them mature.

SINCE 2001 PAM AND I HAVE SERVED AS MISSIONARY evangelists and our main assignment is to teach and train pastors and leaders from rural areas in developing countries of the world. The majority of our work right now is taking place in Kenya East Africa through the Revival Now Schools of Ministry. I am passionate about staying focused on ministry in rural areas and trying to help rural pastors stay encouraged and grow their hearts so He can grow their ministries.

ANOTHER GREAT LESSON I LEARNED IN ALL MY DIFFERENT

ministry assignments is just because you are small doesn't mean you cannot learn to do things with a spirit of excellence. I have heard people in every country of the world I have traveled to complain at times about big churches, all in frustration over the fact that their ministry is not growing as fast as the big church across town. Or like they thought it should. Or would.

IN EVERY MINISTRY ASSIGNMENT I HAVE TAKEN, PAM AND I began with just a hand full of people...or no people at all! You must learn to be thankful where you are now in your assignments, on the way to where you are going.

IN THIS PARABLE OF THE TALENTS TWO OF THOSE THREE MEN who was given the different pieces of money had two distinguishing characteristics: they were thankful; and they were faithful.

IN THE VERY EARLY DAYS OF OUR MINISTRY, SOMEONE GAVE ME a recording of the late John Osteen speaking at a ministers conference at Lakewood Church in Houston, Texas. It was a cassette that powerfully impacted my thinking about ministry; and continues to impact me today. But all I remember from that recording was one thought he hammered home:

"...BE FAITHFUL IN THE SILENT YEARS...WHEN NO ONE IS watching...when no one knows your name. If you can't be faithful in and with the small things, God will never give you greater things.

• *John Osteen*

LIFE IS A LONG JOURNEY OF TWEAKING AND DEFINING YOUR current assignment. It's also a journey through cycles & seasons. It will always be a journey of faithfulness. The will of God will take you through seasons in which you will feel like the heavens are continually open; the anointing and the Glory so heavy on your life you will think you are invisible. Then the will of God will take you through seasons of silence, through hard and harsh circumstances that are actually qualifying and preparing you for greater responsibility in the Kingdom of God. Times in which you can't buy an answer from God nor help from people even if you gave them one million dollars. You will hear those heavy words from Holy Spirit that all of us must heed from time to time: wait. During those silent seasons you must remain faithful to the current assignment because He will not allow you to run away to another place. Don't allow the discouragement of where you are now...your current season...stop you from pursuing where you need to be. In Christ. Closer to God. Full of His Word & Spirit.

I HAVE ALSO FOUND THERE IS A SEASONAL CYCLE WE NEED TO discern about our lives...churches...ministries. Discern those cycles and flow with them and I am convinced we would see a greater measure of fruit and fruitfulness. Be thankful. Be faithful where you are on the way to where you are going. Be faithful in the silent years and silent seasons; the time in which no one is calling on you to minister. Times in which it seems like people are actually blocking you and keeping you from operating in the calling God placed on your life.

GOD HAS ENTRUSTED YOU WITH THE GREATEST CALLING OF all time and will give you many opportunities to have many assignments in your life. But if you are not faithful and thankful for what you currently have and the assignment God has given you now, you may never know the promotion and joy of other assignments God has called you to carry.

CHAPTER THREE

THE MEASURE OF GRACE.

E*phesians 4:7 But unto every one of us is given grace according to the measure of the gift of Christ.*

Act 13:43 Now when the congregation was broken up, many of the Jews and religious proselytes followed Paul and Barnabas: who, speaking to them, persuaded them to continue in the grace of God.

Act 14:26 And thence sailed to Antioch, from whence they had been recommended to the grace of God for the work which they fulfilled.

Act 15:40 And Paul chose Silas, and departed, being recommended by the brethren unto the grace of God.

Romans 12:3 For I say, through the grace given unto me, to every man that is among you, not to think *of himself* more highly than he ought to think; but to think soberly, according as God hath dealt to every man the measure of faith. (Emphasis mine)

I find it very fascinating that Luke, the writer of the Book of Acts describes the work of God "The Grace"

When you submitted your life to Jesus Christ, you received the measure of faith. Directly connected to that measure of faith is what I call the measure of grace. This grace is not the saving grace, but it's the grace for the calling and assignments God will have you do over the course of your lifetime. Every human being that is born again has received this grace whether you realize it or not.

In discussing this measure of grace, keep in mind that just as there is a measure of grace for each individual believer, there is also a grace each local church has and each God ordained ministry has that no other ministry has. There will be many preachers and teachers that will feed you. Some will encourage you. Some will instruct you. But there will be one particular ministry in which you will receive your grace. Some call them denominations. Others call them Fellowship groups. Still others will be labeled non-denominational, but for all of us there will be a place, a denomination, a fellowship or local church where we will "fit".

It's the same thing when you are searching for the distinct difference between your call and your assignment. As we have stated previously, there will be a general call of God upon all our lives; that call is to love the Lord with all our heart, soul, mind, body & strength. Then love our neighbors as ourselves.

Then further, there will be others with specific calls upon them who will recognize God is calling them to serve him in some type of leadership capacity as a layperson, a bi-vocational minister and some as a full-time minister.

Grace is a hot topic in Christianity these days. For some, it's almost as if grace was just invented in 2010. Grace has been around since the very beginning of time. But since Jesus, God our Father has brought grace to the forefront and is now the basis of our salvation and relationship with Him.

Eph 2:8 For by grace are ye saved through faith; and that not of yourselves: *it is* the gift of God:

Eph 2:9 Not of works, lest any man should boast.

Eph 2:10 For we are his workmanship, created in Christ Jesus unto good works, which God hath before ordained that we should walk in them.

Grace has been defined as the unmerited love and favor of God. God gave us Jesus to believe in and through faith in Him, His finished work on Calvary we can be saved from eternal separation from Him. Not by works that we can do so no one would ever be able to brag about the great works their have accomplished to earn salvation.

My definition of grace when it comes to finding your place in His Body is:

"A Divine distribution of God's ability to be who He has called us to be, do what He has called us to do, have what He has called us to have and to accomplish what He has called us to accomplish."

Grace will not only save you...heal you...fill you with His Holy Spirit...

Grace will connect you to a spiritual father/mother and to a company of believers...

And grace will help you understand your call and discover your assignment.

Ephesians 4 tells us there is a distribution of grace given through the five-fold ministry that is released

- To complete
- To build up
- To unify
- To mature
- To increase

This is a distribution that comes only from God above. You cannot buy your way into this grace. You cannot earn your way into this grace. Mama cannot call you, the preacher cannot call you and your earthly father cannot buy you a place in this type of Kingdom leadership. This grace according to Ephesians 4:7 is the gift of Christ.

Whatever assignment God is calling you to operate in right now will come with a leadership grace to be there and do that particular assignment. Over the years I have watched as men have pastored churches, even saw a measure of success, only to have them tell me time and again, "I don't like people, I don't know why I am doing this!" I am not God; but why are you in ministry if you don't even like people? I question whether these kinds of people actually carry the grace to be in that place of ministry. Actually, I think they have chosen this as a career and not a calling. When God calls you and gives you a certain assignment, He will give you grace for that place and a love for the people or the work you are doing.

While this small book doesn't give me the time and space to do a thorough examination of the five ministry gifts listed here in Ephesians 4, I do want to address a couple of things. A great travesty I have seen in every country of the world I have ministered in is when a man or woman is called to the ministry, we automatically assume they are called to be a pastor. But the pastor is not the only leadership gift God has anointed to serve the local church. We have pressured many talented and highly anointed people to accept assignments that were not part of the call of God for their lives because our denominational mindsets have concluded the only "relevant" ministry for the local church is the position of a pastor.

So we "hire" a pastor to come lead us. Work for us. Do all our praying, do all the teaching, do all the preaching, do all the leading, do all the hospital visits and anything and everything that needs to be accomplished so we can have a nice little church. When a man or woman of God carries an anointing that is different from a pastoral anointing and we force them (or entice them with money) to accept an assignment just so they can be in ministry it will not be long before that man or woman will become frustrated, angry, burn out and possibly even leave the ministry all together.

I also am keenly aware there are many men and women who want to be in full-time ministry so bad, they will do anything and take any position, just to be able to say they are in full-time ministry. This is prostitution and harlotry in its simplest form. Someone has to stand up and say this is wrong and it must stop! I'm convinced this is the spirit of Balaam Jesus rebuked the church at Pergamos about in Revelation 2:14:

14 But I have a few things against you, because you have there those who hold the doctrine of Balaam, who taught Balak to put a stumbling block before the children of Israel, to eat things sacrificed to idols, and to commit sexual immorality.

Balaam taught Balak to slowly seduce the children of Israel away from total surrender to the Lordship of Yahweh. In doing so, they began to intermarry with the Midianites and they brought the wrath of God upon the nation.

If God has called you to be an evangelist and you are pastoring simply for the security of receiving a guaranteed payday every week, you need to stop, resign and do it right now! You are out of the will of God pure and simple. What will eventually happen over time, your gift will become frustrated and you will begin to blame people for being rebellious and religious when it is actually you who is out of the will of God. The same thing goes for having a calling to be a teacher, a prophet or an apostle.

I fully understand that sometimes times God will have

you serve in a seasonal assignment such as a staff pastor, music minister, children's worker or something else in order to help you gain experience and understanding of church function and polity that will be an asset to you in a future assignment. Faithfully serving another man or woman's ministry should always equip you to be able to handle more responsibility in God's Kingdom.

The greatest indicator you are in the perfect will of God in this season's assignment is there will be great grace to be where you are and do what is required during this season.

Something that we have missed in understanding our assignment is that this grace I am talking about it's also limited; or it comes in a measure. Salvation grace is NEVER limited. But in your Kingdom work assignment you must identify the grace on your life and stay within the boundaries of what God has called you to do. While we receive the same measure in the beginning, not everyone receives the same grace.

Grace **never** discriminates according to race, age or gender: the grace of God will discriminate according to calling.

1 Corinthians 12:11 *But all these worketh that one and the selfsame Spirit, dividing to every man severally as he will.* KJV

The New King James Version reads this way: *"But one and the same Spirit works all these things, distributing to each one individually as He wills."*

The Amplified reads this way: *"All these [gifts, achievements, abilities] are inspired and brought to pass by one and the same [Holy] Spirit, Who apportions to each person individually [exactly] as He chooses."*

There is a grace from God that is your own personal gift from Jesus to be who He has called you to be, to do what He has called you to do, to have and to accomplish all God planned for your life from the foundation of the world!

The grace that is on my life is not on any other pastor's life. The grace that is on my life is different than any other evangelist or missionary's life in the whole world.

I have become greatly aware that the grace that is on my life...a measure of it is on my wife Pam's life to go with me; but not to the level it is on me. There is a grace for Pam to be Mrs. David Copeland, and no other woman on the earth would be able to function as my wife!

I am often accused of being driven and needy as if the reason I travel and preach so much is that I am trying to meet some need in my life that I have not allowed God to fill. That's not it. The general call on my life is to preach the Gospel. But my assignment for this hour is to travel whenever and wherever He opens the door for me to go. After many, many years of waiting, studying, preparing, my assignment is to go unless He absolutely says NO!

It's not a drivenness or even a mandate: it's a grace! It's a divine distribution of Gods ability...

to be who He has called me to be

do what He called me to do

Go where He called me to go

Say what He has called me to say

to endure what He has called me to endure

To have what He is calling me to have...

And accomplish what He has called me to accomplish;

AND to sow the seeds for future generations and future harvests that ONLY the grace on me can sow.

One plants...one waters...God gives the increase. And we have all entered into other men's labors.

When I was a youth pastor, there was a grace on my life to be a youth pastor.

When I was in radio, there was a grace on my life to be involved in every aspect of Christian radio. When I was a music minister,, there was a grace for that assignment.

When I was a lead pastor, there was a grace to be planted in one place, to be deeply involved with people in one location. Now, there is a grace on me to go to the nations of the world!

I am convinced God wants to release into your life a fresh grace for you to be who He has called you to be; do what He has called you to do; to have what He has called you to have and to accomplish all He has called you to accomplish.

There is fresh grace for families and marriages to be healed and to flourish. There is a fresh grace on businessmen and businesswoman to make money and be a resource for Kingdom ministry.

There is a fresh grace for others to step into politics for God surely knows we need men and women of character and integrity serving in the public arena!

Whatever it is that is in your heart to accomplish for God, there will be a grace to excel, to accelerate and accomplish His assignment for your life.

Our challenge is to discern the grace on our lives, flow in that grace on our lives and trust God to increase the grace as needed for the challenges ahead.

What is the grace on your life? How do we discern the grace?

Discerning the grace upon your life will enable you to identify the assignment on your life.

1.The grace on your life will bring faith hope and love to others!

Again, Look at Eph 4:11-17

[11] And He Himself gave some *to be* apostles, some prophets, some evangelists, and some pastors and teachers, [12] for the equipping of the saints for the work of ministry, for the edifying of the body of Christ, [13] till we all come to the unity of the faith and of the knowledge of the

Son of God, to a perfect man, to the measure of the stature of the fullness of Christ; [14] that we should no longer be children, tossed to and fro and carried about with every wind of doctrine, by the trickery of men, in the cunning craftiness of deceitful plotting, [15] but, speaking the truth in love, may grow up in all things into Him who is the head—Christ — [16] from whom the whole body, joined and knit together by what every joint supplies, according to the effective working by which every part does its share, causes growth of the body for the edifying of itself in love.

So the whole purpose of the five-fold ministry is:

- To equip
- To complete
- To build up
- To unify
- To mature
- To increase

When this happens, faith will come into people's hearts, hope will be restored to broken lives, and love will be our entire motivation for ministry as it should have been from the beginning!

2.The grace on your life will bring joy to you and others.

The grace will produce joy!

Isaiah 55:12 For you shall go out with joy and be led forth with peace: the mountains and the hills shall break forth before you into singing, and all the trees of the field shall clap their hands.

Every time there has been a change of assignments for me and Pam, it has ALWAYS been marked with great joy. Not just the joy of knowing you are in the center of His will for your everyday life; I call this every day joy. But a joy that (as the old song says) is unspeakable and full of Glory! Knowing in your inner man you are following the will of God for your life brings unspeakable and unexplainable joy; in spite of any sacrifice or hardship involved!

3.Grace will increase as we walk in it...and speak it forth...

This speaks to obedience.

Col 4:6 Let your speech be always with grace, seasoned with salt, that ye may know how ye ought to answer every man.

For some, what our Father is calling us into is going to make us feel like we are drowning. It will definitely pull us out of our comfort zone. God will never call you to do something when you have enough money, have enough time, or even have enough experience. He will use the opportunity to teach you as you go.

This will cause us to feel outside our pay grade or skill set. But there is a fresh grace available to

Be who He called us to be

do what He called us to do

Go where He called us to go

Say what He has called us to say

Endure what He has called us to endure

Have what He has called us to have

And accomplish what He has called us to accomplish...

4.The last marker in discerning the grace on our lives will be peace.

Again, Isaiah 55:12 For you shall go out with joy and be led forth with peace: the mountains and the hills shall break forth before you into singing, and all the trees of the field shall clap their hands.

Colossians 3:15 *15 And let the peace of God rule in your hearts, to which also you were called in one body; and be thankful.*

The word rule as it is used here literally means *"to be an umpire*". In American Baseball, when an umpire says you are out, you're out. If the umpire says you are safe, the opposing coach (or the devil) cannot disqualify you from your assignment.

Whatever assignment God calls you to whether a pastor, missionary, apostle, prophet; a business man or business woman, a doctor, lawyer, mechanic, housewife or farmer...

There IS grace for your place.

CHAPTER FOUR

ACTIVATING YOU MEASURE OF GRACE

In a previous chapter we discussed how that when we are born again, every human being is given the measure of faith. Attached to that measure of faith (Romans 12:3) is a measure of grace to grow that faith and accomplish what you were put on earth to do.

AGAIN, LOOK AT EPHESIANS 4:7:

BUT UNTO EVERY ONE OF US IS GIVEN GRACE ACCORDING TO THE measure of the gift of Christ.

THIS MEASURE OF GRACE IS A DIVINE DISTRIBUTION OF GOD'S ability to be who He called us to be; do what he called us to do; have what He called us to have; and accomplish what He called us to accomplish. The anointing we currently operate in is directly connected to the measure of grace distributed into our lives. It is also connected to the measure of faith we have allowed God and His Word to build in us. When you see someone operate in a strong anointing or with strong faith, what you don't see is how they have spent many years in obscurity, being faithful, applying God's Word to situations they were facing. But it all started with the same measure of faith everyone receives when they are born again.

The word *measure* comes from the Greek word *metron* which is the same word we get our English word "meter." By implication it is a limited degree; and determined extent, portion, something measured off; a limit. Again, the grace of God that saves us, heals us, delivers us is unlimited in scope and duration. The measure of grace for your assignment will be limited to the work HE has called us to do.

WE MUST NEVER ATTEMPT TO WORK OUTSIDE OUR MEASURE of grace. When you do you are asking for frustration, difficulty and certain failure. But if we are faithful to stay within the measure of our assignment, the peace and mercy of God will always be with us, even during difficult circumstances.

BEAR IN MIND, GOD IS THE ONE THAT DISTRIBUTES THE measure. He has every right to limit our assignment or to broaden our assignment. He has every right to call me to Kenya, or to limit my assignment to a small city in Alabama. This is HIS work, not ours! Jesus told His disciples:

. . .

YOU DID NOT CHOOSE ME, BUT I CHOSE YOU AND APPOINTED you that you should go and bear fruit, and *that* your fruit should remain, that whatever you ask the Father in My name He may give you. John 15:16 NKJV

FIVE WAYS THIS GRACE IS ACTIVATED

I KNOW I AM REPEATING MYSELF, BUT KEEP IN MIND, THIS IS the grace to be, do, have and accomplish what God put us on the earth to be, do, have, and accomplish. This grace will be activated in the following ways:

I. INTIMACY.

Intimacy with God will always give us power with men. Look at Jesus words in Matthew 7:21-23:

"NOT EVERYONE WHO SAYS TO ME, 'LORD, LORD,' SHALL ENTER the kingdom of heaven, but he who does the will of My Father in heaven. 22 Many will say to Me in that day, 'Lord, Lord, have we not prophesied in Your name, cast out demons in Your name, and done many wonders in Your name?' 23 And then I will declare to them, 'I never knew you; depart from Me, you who practice lawlessness!' NKJV

INTIMACY IS SOMETHING DONE IN PRIVATE BETWEEN A husband and wife that are deeply in love with each other. It happens behind closed doors where all barriers can be removed. Intimacy is not something everyone has authority or the privilege to see.

. . .

IN MY OPINION, ONE OF THE REASONS PORNOGRAPHY HAS such a powerful hold on people is it gives people access to something that should be private and concealed. It's a secret that should only be reserved for a husband and wife. When it is put on the internet,, it captures our attention because we know we are seeing something that should be seen or done in a private setting.

OUR PUBLIC LIFE WILL BE EITHER STRENGTHENED OR destroyed by our private life. What we do in private determines how we act in public. From the secret place of prayer, intimacy with God accomplishes four things:

1.IT FOCUSES ME. ONE OF THE GREAT CHALLENGES IN MY LIFE is to stay focused. There is not a person reading this book that doesn't have to fight distractions. Intimacy with God in the secret place of prayer helps us focus on the most important things about our assignment.

2.INTIMACY FILLS ME. TIME WITH JESUS HELPS US TO EMPTY ourselves of our agenda and fills me with His agenda!

3.INTIMACY FORTIFIES ME. I HAVE NEVER SPENT TIME IN HIS Presence when He didn't touch me and strengthen me in some way. Time spent in His Presence is never wasted.

4.INTIMACY FREES ME. INTIMACY WITH JESUS WILL ALWAYS SET me free to remember I am a son of the Most High God and I belong to Him. He trusts me enough to call me to follow Him then frees me from the religious mindsets that keep me from embracing and walking out my assignment for Him!

II. INTERCESSION WILL ACTIVATE GRACE FOR YOUR assignment.

JESUS SPENT MANY NIGHTS PRAYING ALL NIGHT TO THE Father. Those times of intercession equipped Jesus to be able to instantly obey the voice of His Father. When daybreak came, He was so in tune with what Father God wanted, He never got confused about what He was leading Him to do that particular day, or with any particular situation.

III. WORSHIP ACTIVATES GRACE FOR YOUR ASSIGNMENT.

WORSHIP HAS NOTHING TO DO WITH A STYLE OF MUSIC OR A method of preaching & teaching the Word of God. It has everything to do with the attitude of our heart. I'm not sure who said it but this is what worship means to me:

WORSHIP IS LOVE POURED OUT EXTRAVAGANTLY;
For worship to be worship, it must have an object; and the value of the object determines the value of your worship.

. . .

I'M NOT TALKING ABOUT WORSHIPPING BECAUSE YOUR favorite song is being played at church. You attitude concerning the style of music being sung or played has a direct connection with what you will receive from that service.

SOME TIME AGO WHILE IN PRAYER, HOLY SPIRIT WHISPERED TO me, "son, you have spent the majority of your life and ministry operating out of the soulish realm and not the Spirit realm..." Upon closer inspection of my heart I had to agree. I began to remember some messages I have preached at different times when in reality I was angry, frustrated or wanted to prove I had more Bible knowledge than someone who was attacking me.

MAN, DID I EVER REPENT!

BUT IT ALSO SET ME ON A JOURNEY TO LEARN TO OPERATE out of my spirit and not my own mind, will or emotions.

WHAT HAPPENS WHEN SOMEONE AT CHURCH SINGS A CHORUS you really don't care for, verses when someone sings a hymn? The Holy Spirit is not limited to moving only when Southern Gospel songs are being sung. And for the younger crowd, He doesn't stop moving when we stop singing something that Bethel has not produced!

HOW YOU REACT AND RESPOND WHEN A CERTAIN STYLE OF

music is being sung will reveal your true worship. How you respond to someone who teaches or preaches in a different style that what you are used to will reveal your true worship and the level of maturity in your life.

IV.PRAYING IN TONGUES WILL ACTIVATE YOUR MEASURE OF grace.

1 CORINTHIANS 14:2 "**2** FOR HE WHO SPEAKS IN A TONGUE does not speak to men but to God, for no one understands *him;* however, in the spirit he speaks mysteries."

HUMAN BEINGS ARE COMPRISED OF THREE PARTS: WE ARE spirit beings, we have a soul (our mind, our will and our emotions) and we live our lives on this earth in fleshly body that is still subject to being attacked with sickness, disease and difficulties.

WHEN YOU GAVE YOUR LIFE TO JESUS CHRIST, IT WAS YOUR spirit that was born anew. That doesn't mean we become so close to God nothing can ever touch us anymore; no! In fact, the closer you draw to Jesus, the more bizarre attacks will come. The more you activate and understand the measure of grace upon your life, Satan will attempt to either distract you from your assignment or destroy you so you cannot complete your assignment.

. . .

YOUR SPIRIT ALREADY KNOWS THE FULL MEASURE OF WHAT your assignment entails. Your spirit knows things your mind cannot receive. When I was born again, I was told in a prophetic word that I would touch the nations of the world. At that time, my spirit knew it; it bore witness that the word was from God; but my mind could not understand how God would take a sixteen-year-old boy like me and move Him around the world preaching the Gospel.

BUT THE MORE I STUDIED THE WORD, THE MORE I PRAYED, the more I worshipped Him in the secret place, and the more I prayed in other tongues, the more my mind would yield to the measure of faith that was connected to the measure of grace already on my life.

WHICH LEADS ME TO THE LAST POINT IN ACTIVATING THE measure of grace:

V.THE GIFT OF PROPHECY WILL ACTIVATE THE MEASURE OF grace in your life.

PAUL TOLD HIS SPIRITUAL SON TIMOTHY IN 1 TIMOTHY 1:18:

THIS CHARGE I COMMIT TO YOU, SON TIMOTHY, ACCORDING TO the prophecies previously made concerning you, that by them you may wage the good warfare.... NKJV

. . .

YOU MAY BE READING THIS BOOK AND THINK, I DON'T BELIEVE God still speaks like that to people! Maybe your church doesn't believe and teach that personal prophecy is for today. Or maybe you are a part of a ministry that believes and practices it, but there have been so many weird things that have happened surrounding personal prophecy that has turned you against this spiritual gift.

I SERVED IN A MAJOR PENTECOSTAL DENOMINATION FOR OVER twenty-three years, and I was always taught when it came to personal prophetic words that you should just put them "on the shelf" and if it was really a word from God, it would come to pass. But Paul's instruction to Timothy flies in the face of that thinking!

PAUL COMMANDED TIMOTHY TO *WAR WITH THE WORDS THAT had been spoken over his life.*

1 TIMOTHY 1:18 "THIS CHARGE I COMMIT UNTO THEE, SON Timothy, according to the prophecies which went before on thee, that thou by them mightest war a good warfare;" KJV

THE NEW LIVING TRANSLATION SAYS IT THIS WAY:

"TIMOTHY, MY SON, HERE ARE MY INSTRUCTIONS FOR YOU, BASED on the prophetic words spoken about you earlier. May they help you fight well in the Lord's battles."

. . .

MANY YEARS AGO, DORIS DAY RECORDED A SONG THAT SAID "...whatever will be, will be..." That has become the way so many people live when it concerns understanding the measure of grace for their assignment. God is not trying to keep you in the dark. He is NOT attempting to disqualify you from running your race and grasping your assignment you were put on earth to do. NO! He is the same Lord Who said,

PRAY THAT THE LORD OF THE HARVEST WILL SEND FORTH *laborers into His harvest* Matthew 9:38 (my paraphrase)

THERE WILL BE SOME PROPHETIC WORDS THAT MAY NOT BEAR witness with your spirit. There WILL be words that are NOT from God but they are from the minds of men that are wanting to encourage us. There will be other words that might even confuse us. Those that confuse you, simply throw them out of your mind and reject them totally.

BUT THERE WILL BE WORDS THAT WILL BE SPOKEN OVER YOUR life at different seasons that WILL be from God, but won't resonate with you at the time. As you pray over them or pray into them, God will reveal whether or not this is a word that you need to war your warfare with. I have started keeping a record (as much as possible) of the personal prophetic words people speak over my life. Because just maybe, even though my mind cannot comprehend something now, doesn't mean God is not trying to stretch my faith for something He is wanting to do down the road.

. . .

Just because your mind can't receive it at the moment doesn't mean it's not God speaking to you.

Hold on to and learn to war with the promises God makes to you either through the written word or personal prophecy.

CHAPTER FIVE

IDENTIFY, ACCEPT & EMBRACE YOUR MEASURE
OF GRACE

In activating our measure of grace there are several steps to consider in order to thoroughly understand our assignment:

1.Identify your measure of grace.

When you think about answering the calling of God for your life, the greatest fear people will battle is a fear that God will ask them to sell everything they have, move to a far-off country, where they will never see their loved ones ever again. Let me tell you for sure, whatever God has prepared for your life, there will be a desire to accomplish that very thing. He will give you a desire for your assignment.

Identifying your assignment will take some sincere honesty on your part. It may require some fasting and prayer seeking His face for clarity over your assignment. It may also require you to seek out some honest assessment from spiritual fathers and mothers of the faith.

I always recommend people make a list of things that are burning in their hearts to do for God. When you do that and as you seek Him to clarify, He will help eliminate the items that need to be discarded. The crème of what the Father has called you to do will always rise to the top of your list.

If God has called you to serve as a pastor, He will give you an overwhelming desire to settle in one location and connect with one local fellowship. I feel very strongly He will not only give you a desire to be in one city, He will also CALL you to a certain city. With our nation in the spiritual condition it is in we absolutely need men and women to be called to a city or town and not just a church. I've seen in my life many men and women called to a church, only because it paid well or had a wonderful benefit package. Oh, that men and women would surrender to the calling of God to be in a city and not just a large church with a nice benefits package!

If God has called you to travel as an evangelist, a singer, an itinerant missionary, stop trying to pastor simply for the security of receiving a check every week. As I have already stated previously, this is prostitution of the Divine distribution of grace upon your life.

If God has called you to be a children's pastor, youth pastor, or even to serve as an associate, be someone's number two man; don't be afraid to accept and embrace that as your assignment from heaven. There is ALWAYS grace for your place.

2. Second, you must accept your measure of grace.

This was always something I thought I did, until I realized one day, I was complaining to God about promotion not coming to me. I spent many years attempting to fit in certain denominations and different streams of the Holy Spirit expression, only to be frustrated that people acted like I wasn't even in the room. Thankfully, Holy Spirit showed me the reason I didn't "fit" was because that was not part of my assignment.

Ouch. Yes, it stung. It hurt me deeply. But it was also liberating. That pressure to attempt to fit into a particular structure or fellowship group actually was distracting me from the very people who needed the Divine distribution of grace that was on my life.

I didn't realize, all those years I was belittling, complaining and constantly comparing the anointing and grace upon my life with others, had actually hindered the flow of anointing that could operate through me. The day I actually repented of the comparison and complaining sin, there was freedom that surged through me that I cannot explain in words.

I am reminded of an episode in Peter's life in John 21 that sums up what I am trying to convey when I say accept your measure of grace.

John 21:20 Then Peter, turning around, saw the disciple whom Jesus loved following, who also had leaned on His breast at the supper, and said, "Lord, who is the one who betrays You?" 21 Peter, seeing him, said to Jesus, "But Lord, what *about* this man?"

22 Jesus said to him, "If I [h]will that he remain till I come, what *is that* to you? You follow Me."

Jesus has just pointedly asked Peter three different times did He love Him. Each time Peter responded you can feel the potential embarrassment on Peter. I can imagine him saying to himself secretly, "Come on Jesus! Why do you keep asking me this question?"

In an effort to deflect the attention off himself, he looks at John and says, "...well what about him?"

Jesus responds very clearly in paraphrase and says, "that's none of your business! You follow Me!"

At one time or another, you will be tempted to live the comparison game. Comparing your ministry, anointing, and ministry style to someone else who looks like their ministry is more powerful, or more successful than yours is a trap Satan will keep you in bondage to for a long time. That is a deadly game and will lead to nothing but constant heartache and bitterness.

Back in the late 1990s as I was pastoring in East Alabama, it seemed like every church was experiencing a special season of outpouring. During that time there were some families who left our church and went to a couple of other churches who looked as if they were actually having a "greater move of God" than we were. I found myself in a spiritual battle with the accuser of the brethren (that manifested through disgruntled people) that seemed to be tearing down everything we were attempting to do in our effort of following Jesus' leadership. Even though I know for sure these pastors would never attack our ministry, I still was frustrated and hurt because these disgruntled people made it look as if these pastors were actively recruiting people from our church.

One Friday afternoon while in prayer for the Sunday service, I had just received word that another couple from our church was leaving our ministry to go to the church that had a "real pastor" who was really "moving with the Spirit". Needless to say, I was somewhat devastated. But not surprised. I had been fasting and praying for some time, asking God to reveal to me why I couldn't flow with that same type of anointing. Suddenly, I had a brilliant idea: I would pray for God to pour out His Spirit in a tremendous way and use them in our town to bring a massive outpouring of the Spirit we desperately needed.

After praying that way for a few minutes, Holy Spirit stopped me and whispered ever so gently to me and said, "...

do you realize what you are asking me to do? What if I give revival to them and not to you? Are you going to be ok with that?"

I fell to my knees in the parsonage in which we were living at the time and I began to weep and cry and began declaring, "YES! Yes Lord, I will be ok if you give revival to them and not to us, and I will support them as well." Something broke. It broke in me first. And I was sincere in my response to the Lord. For the next hour or so I prayed for those churches for God to really and truly bless them and pour out His Spirit in a tangible way!

Something also broke for our church. Two days later in our Sunday service, we had a breakthrough the church has never has in all the years it had been in existence. Revival broke out. People began to give their lives to Jesus. Every Sunday was like a brand new revival! Healings, deliverances, marriages restored.

I stopped comparing my ministry and judging our success by what others were doing. I accepted my measure of grace. And I've never been the same since.

Someone is reading this book right now, and you have been judging and disqualifying the way God uses you with how He uses others. Stop. Stop it. Stop it right now!

You are the only you there will ever be in this life. When you learn to appreciate, identify and celebrate the measure of grace you have, there will be a fresh anointing that will flow, and a new dynamic of peace you have never experienced before.

3.Finally you must rest and be faithful in your measure of grace.

Every pastor, every ministry leader in every nation has a working concept, a basic understanding of how God wants them to conduct their ministry. Just because I do ministry a certain way doesn't mean I think this is the only way to do ministry. There have been a lot of unique anointings that have been put on a shelf because many pastors and ministry leaders have given in to the pressure of copying what someone else has done and expect the same success. I know that will work sometimes and to a certain degree. But I can tell you with great certainty, there will come a time in which that will not work anymore. What Works in Lanett, Alabama may not work in Atlanta, Georgia. What works in Los Angeles, California won't work in rural Kilgoris, Kenya. God has given you a distinct measure of grace to accomplish something only you can accomplish. But I can also assure you, the method that DOES work in every city and every nation of the world is hearing from God and obeying what God says to do.

Being faithful over the long term will bring life to many people. As Jesus spoke in the parable of the talents in a previous chapter, He will not judge us with how successful we are in men's eyes; God will judge us by how faithful we are with His Word and in His eyes. It's faithfulness and resting in the measure of grace He has given you that will allow His peace, joy, assurance and contentment to shine forth to others.

There is grace for your place.

CHAPTER SIX

FOURTEEN LESSONS ABOUT YOUR ASSIGNMENT

Life is a long journey of understanding and defining your current assignment. We have attempted to establish in this book there is a general call of God that will rest upon your life until you die. But there will be different assignments at different seasons of your life.

Some assignments will only last a short time. You will take elements (and experiences) of your current assignment into future seasons of different assignments. The following points are just some of the things I have learned in my lifetime in both grappling with and grasping my assignment. Feel free to use them as a small group study guide. Or simply make a list of these points and feel free to add to the list those points Holy Spirit will speak to you about your life assignments:

. . .

1. YOUR ASSIGNMENT IS DIRECTLY CONNECTED TO THE
passion in your heart.

Many people are afraid to surrender to the call of God
because they are afraid of having to give up a lifestyle of
material things they have gotten used to.

GOD WILL GIVE YOU A DESIRE TO DO WHAT YOUR ASSIGNMENT
is. Think about this. Let it settle deep in your inner man.
God WILL give you a desire to do what His assignment for
your life is!

WHILE THERE IS A CROSS OF SELF DENIAL WE MUST ALL CARRY
and some responsibilities within our assignments we won't
necessarily like, He will give us a desire and a passion to do
what He's calling us to do.

MANY RELIGIOUS PEOPLE HAVE MADE PASSION A BAD THING.
But you will only be successful at something you are
passionate about.

2.GODS ASSIGNMENT FOR YOUR LIFE WILL REQUIRE FAITH.

God won't tell you to take every single step you already
know you should be taking (you should already be doing
it): but He will lead you to take a step. And that step will
always require faith

YOUR ASSIGNMENT WILL ALWAYS REQUIRE FAITH...STEPS OF
faith. Years ago I was complaining about it being so hard.
God spoke very clearly and said "there will never be a time

in which you won't need faith: but I will always meet you at the point of your obedience".

MANY PEOPLE SPEAK OF TAKING LEAPS OF FAITH TO FOLLOW Him in their assignment. But God will NEVER direct you to take a leap of faith. But He will lead you to steps of faith.

PSALMS 37:23 THE STEPS OF A *GOOD* MAN ARE [D]ORDERED BY the Lord,
And He delights in his way.

3.YOUR ASSIGNMENT WILL HAVE DIFFERENT FUNCTIONS AT different seasons.

In the early days of our ministry we had a very good friend named Jim Holland. He always knew I was called to itinerant ministry and he wanted me to be an evangelist from the time I met him in 1981. I also knew I was called to this current assignment; but every time I prayed about making that step, I could hear the Holy Spirit say *wait!*

YOUR WORK WILL CHANGE FROM TIME TO TIME AS YOU ARE faithful to the current assignment that God has given to you.

FINALLY, AFTER MANY YEARS OF SERVING IN PASTORAL ministry, Holy Spirit released me from that assignment to pursue full time traveling ministry: an assignment I knew I was called to in 1978 when I accepted the call to ministry. Every assignment from God has a timing: if we lag behind in God's timing we may never fulfill what the perfect will of

God is for our lives. If we get ahead of Him we may end up aborting His plans because of the stress of being out of sync with His timing. Being out of His timing doesn't mean you are out of His will. If you are out of His timing, it tends to cause great chaos, not only for our lives but also in the lives of others.

4.YOUR ASSIGNMENT WILL BE TO SPECIFIC PEOPLE...AT specific times...maybe even for specific reasons. There will be a grace to be there...

In the 1980's I was specifically given the assignment to pastor youth. In the early 1990's it was music and being an associate pastor...learning to serve another man's vision. Oftentimes you will have to serve another man's vision before you will ever see others support your own.

From 1995-2001 my assignment was to be a Lead Pastor in our hometown of Lanett, Alabama. I could see myself pastoring that church the rest of my life. In fact, in each position I have been in (with each Assignment) I could see myself doing that the rest of my life.

IN 2001, I BEGAN TO TRAVEL AS AN EVANGELIST...NOW AS A Missionary, to many pastors and churches in Kenya, Tanzania and many other countries of the world. I could not do what I am doing now in 1978 when God first called me to preach the Gospel. But little by little, step by step, I embraced the assignment I was given. Little did I know then, the faithfulness to that assignment in those days, became the training ground for what we are doing today through the Revival Now Schools of Ministry across East Africa.

. . .

AGAIN....LIFE IS A LONG JOURNEY OF DISCOVERING AND defining your current assignment. It will be to specific people, at specific times and for specific reasons.

5.YOUR ASSIGNMENT <u>WILL</u> BE GEOGRAPHICAL. A SPECIFIC place. That May change from time to time.

WHERE YOU ARE GEOGRAPHICALLY IS JUST AS IMPORTANT AS where you are spiritually. If your assignment from God is in Tennessee and you are in California, there won't be a grace for you to be and do, and have, and accomplish what you would if you were in the correct geographical location.

I WOULD LOVE TO PREACH IN LARGE CHURCHES NEAR LARGE airports every week. I would love to stay in the nicest hotels and have all my expenses always provided for me in advance. I'm not being jealous or critical or envious: I recognize my assignment is to smaller churches in rural and often remote locations of the United States as well as the world.

I ESPECIALLY KNOW WITHOUT A DOUBT THAT AS OF THE writing of this book, our main assignment is to East Africa, especially the nation of Kenya. You don't get to choose the location; the location chooses you!

6.YOUR ASSIGNMENT WILL REQUIRE YOUR TOTAL FOCUS.

In the story of Elijah & Elisha, Elijah says to Elisha:

2KINGS 2:10 AND HE SAID, THOU HAST ASKED A HARD THING: nevertheless, if thou see me when I am taken from thee, it shall be so unto thee; but if not, it shall not be so. KJV

MEN OF ELIJAH'S DAY HAD THE SAME PROBLEM MEN AND women have today: staying focused!

SOMEONE HAS STATED THAT WE ARE BOMBARDED WITH WELL over 35,000 different messages every single day. With social media, it wouldn't surprise me to find out it's much more than that. It also would be safe to say the average person will hear one thousand different voices demanding his or her attention each and every day.

THE FIGHT OF OUR LIFETIME IS THE FIGHT TO STAY FOCUSED on our assignment. Not only will the devil attempt to distract us, family, friends and well-meaning people may try to distract you away from giving your total focus to your assignment.

EVERY WEEK SOMEWHERE IN THE UNITED STATES, SOMEONE will ask me, "Copeland, when are you going to stop wasting your time traveling around the world? When are you going to settle down and pastor again?"

I ALWAYS TELL PEOPLE, "I WILL SETTLE DOWN AND STOP

traveling so much when I get old, discouraged and want to disobey the assignment God has for my life!"

WHICH LEADS ME TO NUMBER 7:

7.YOUR ASSIGNMENT WILL REQUIRE YOUR COMPLETE obedience.

I Samuel 15:22,23 22 And Samuel said, Hath the Lord as great delight in burnt offerings and sacrifices, as in obeying the voice of the Lord? Behold, to obey is better than sacrifice, and to hearken than the fat of rams.

23 FOR REBELLION IS AS THE SIN OF WITCHCRAFT, AND stubbornness is as iniquity and idolatry. Because thou hast rejected the word of the Lord, he hath also rejected thee from being king.

DON'T TRY TO EXPLAIN THE REASON YOU ARE DOING WHAT you are doing to everybody...they will try to talk you out of it. *Your assignment will require your complete obedience*

DON'T TRY TO BE LIKE EVERYONE ELSE, NO MATTER HOW COOL or relevant they may be. You were not made to be a replica: you were made to be an original.

PEOPLE WHO DO NOT RESPECT YOUR ANOINTING AND YOUR assignment will never accept or respect your time or your advice

. . .

YOUR ASSIGNMENT WILL REQUIRE YOUR TOTAL AND COMPLETE
obedience.

**8.YOUR ASSIGNMENT WILL GIVE YOU MANY OPPORTUNITIES TO
be offended.**

In Genesis 26 we find the story of Isaac & Abimelech.
Abimelech was so jealous of the success and prosperity
Isaac had on his life for simply embracing his assignment
from God. God commanded Isaac to sow seed in an obscure
land and in an inconvenient time in which people and
circumstances were not conducive to economic development and prosperity. Abimelech eventually chased him
away from the place God told him to settle.

PEOPLE WILL REJECT YOUR ASSIGNMENT! THEY WILL BE THE
voice of accusation and deem you unqualified. People will
criticize & complain about your assignment because it
doesn't look like real ministry. They will ridicule and drag
your name through the mud. If they can't gossip you into
aborting your assignment, some will even physically fight
you and try to stop you from completing your assignment.

THIS IS SATAN'S ATTEMPTED TO GET YOU OFFENDED AND STOP
the flow of blessings into your life. Finally, Abimelech came
to Isaac at Beersheba and wanted to make peace. Isaac
furnished the covenant meal and released King Abimelech
to return home in peace. That very day, Isaac's servants
found water and they named the place the well of Beersheba; the well of the oath or the well of seven, which

means completion. When you further examine the life of Isaac, you will find he never moved again until the last days of his life when he was moved closer to his burial plot in Mamre.

DON'T ALLOW OTHER PEOPLE'S OFFENSE OVER YOUR assignment drag you into their offense.

9.YOUR ASSIGNMENT WILL DAILY CALL YOU TO DIE TO yourself

Luke 9:23-27

When you are forgotten, or neglected, or purposely set at naught, and you don't sting and hurt with the insult or the over-sight, but your heart is happy, being counted worthy to suffer for Christ, that is dying to self.

WHEN YOUR GOOD IS EVIL SPOKEN OF, WHEN YOUR WISHES ARE crossed, your advice disregarded, your opinions ridiculed, and you refuse to let anger rise in your heart, or even defend yourself, but take it all in patient loving silence, that is dying to self.

WHEN YOU LOVINGLY AND PATIENTLY BEAR ANY DISORDER, ANY irregularity, any unpunctuality, or any annoyance; when you can stand face-to-face with waste, folly, extravagance, spiritual insen-sibility, and endure it as Jesus endured it, that is dying to self.

WHEN YOU ARE CONTENT WITH ANY FOOD, ANY OFFERING, ANY raiment, any climate, any society, any solitude, any interruption by the will of God, that is dying to self. Steve Hill Devotion

. . .

10. YOUR ASSIGNMENT WILL PRODUCE GREAT PEACE AND JOY IN your life

Isaiah 55:11 So shall my word be that goeth forth out of my mouth: it shall not return unto me void, but it shall accomplish that which I please, and it shall prosper in the thing whereto I sent it.

12 **FOR YE SHALL GO OUT WITH JOY, AND BE LED FORTH WITH peace:** the mountains and the hills shall break forth before you into singing, and all the trees of the field shall clap their hands.

13 INSTEAD OF THE THORN SHALL COME UP THE FIR TREE, AND instead of the brier shall come up the myrtle tree: and it shall be to the Lord for a name, for an everlasting sign that shall not be cut off.

COL 3:15 AND LET THE PEACE OF GOD RULE IN YOUR hearts, to which also ye are called in one body; and be ye thankful.

GOD WILL GIVE YOU THE DESIRE TO DO WHAT HE IS CALLING you to do!

11. YOUR ASSIGNMENT WILL NEVER TAKE YOU AWAY FROM prayer and time with The Lord. In fact, the assignment and call of God for you will require a growing prayer life as well as a growing faith.

12. YOUR ASSIGNMENT WILL BE SO BIG YOU WILL NEED OTHERS **to get involved with you to see it fulfilled.**
    You cannot complete your assignment alone!

JOSHUA HAD CALEB. DAVID HAD JONATHAN. JESUS SENT THE disciples out two by two. Many times when you see Peter in Scripture you will see John as well. Paul & Barnabas work together for quite a while and when a disagreement came between them, Paul chose Silas to go with him on his missionary journeys.

YOUR ASSIGNMENT WILL BE SO BIG, YOU WILL ALWAYS NEED the help of others along the way.

13. YOU WILL NEED FAVOR WITH GOD AND FAVOR WITH MAN **to complete your assignment.**
    God will have to connect you to and through open doors and key people to help you with your assignment. I always like to say, you cannot go to heaven when you die without favor with God; and you will never complete your assignment on the earth without favor with man.

14. FOR YOUR ASSIGNMENT/CALLING TO PLEASE GOD IT MUST **flow from the River of God!**
    You MUST have the power of the Holy Spirit to complete your assignment!

. . .

PSALMS 46:4 *THERE IS* A RIVER WHOSE STREAMS SHALL MAKE glad the city of God,

The holy *place* of the [c]tabernacle of the Most High.

5 God *is* in the midst of her, she shall not be [d]moved;

God shall help her, just [e]at the break of dawn.

ACTS 1:8 BUT YOU SHALL RECEIVE POWER WHEN THE HOLY Spirit has come upon you; and you shall be [c]witnesses to Me in Jerusalem, and in all Judea and Samaria, and to the end of the earth."

ACKNOWLEDGMENTS

To my wife Pam; my companion over the last four decades; you have made me a better man and I am grateful to God He gave you to me for this journey. Thank you for being my best earthly friend.

To my editor Adam Davis: thanks for kicking me when I needed it to help me focus on the assignment.

To my daughters Megan & Missy; and their husbands Eric & David: thankfully you guys will never have to experience the pain religion caused me on the way to find my assignment.

To my grandchildren Madison, Elijah, Andrew, Abigail & Asher: I promise I will do all I can to help you find your assignment at a young age, so you don't waste as much time as I have….

To our Revival Now Ministry Partners: Thank you for

believing in and supporting our part of the Great Commission.

To Holy Spirit: thank You for never giving up on me. Thank You for being my constant companion and best friend!

AFTERWORD

I hope this book has been and will continue to be a blessing to you. You have been chosen by God to live in the greatest day in history: today!

I don't want anyone to have to struggle the way I have struggled for so many years, not understanding the difference between my inheritance, my general calling and my seasonal assignments.

If I had known some things I have written here in the early days of my walk with Jesus, I don't think I would have been discouraged so much of the time. I spent many years feeling trapped, tricked by God and overwhelmed by people not understanding that what God had put in my heart was much bigger than my current status or situation. But in every assignment, at every station, God taught me things that could only be learned by walking close to Him. Even when the dream of traveling for His name burned deep within my heart.

If this book has helped you in any way, I would love to hear from you. Not because I need the validation, but because I want to pray for you and your assignment on the earth. You won't always be where you are right now: so enjoy where you are on the way to where you are going!

You can email david@revivalnow.org; or write to

David Copeland
    Revival Now International
    P.O. Box 1076
    Lanett, Alabama 36863

May God bless you and use you for His Kingdom purposes all the days of your life!

ABOUT THE AUTHOR

Dr. David Copeland is founder and director of Revival Now International, a United States-based, no-profit organization, specializing in US and overseas evangelism, leadership equipping and ministry development as well as local church planting.

In 2010 David & Pam established the Revival Now Schools of Ministry in Kilgoris, Kenya; a mobile quarterly ministry development training school specifically geared for rural pastors and leaders and those leaders who have not had the opportunity to attend a formal Bible School. David is also the US Director of the Hope Centre Children's Home in Nyangusu/Kilgoris Kenya, home to approximately 30 orphans from the southwest Kenya region.

David has been ordained to the Gospel ministry since 1983 and has served in various ministry assignments since 1978. He is currently an ordained minister with the Association of Evangelical Gospel Assemblies (AEGA) based in Monroe, Louisiana. David has also served as a Youth Pastor, Associate Pastor, Music Minister, Lead Pastor and since 2001 as a short-term missionary to the nations of the world with his primary emphasis in East Africa.

David has been married to his best friend Pam since 1980 and has two daughters, two sons-in-law and five grandchildren who are the absolute joy of his life; second to Jesus of course!

For More information on Revival Now International, write to us at:

Revival Now International
 P.O. Box 1076
 Lanett, Alabama 36863

Phone 1.706.773.1546
 Email: david@revivalnow.org

Or Visit our website: http://revivalnow.org

facebook.com/RevivalNowInternational
twitter.com/DavidCopeland
instagram.com/revivalnow

CPSIA information can be obtained
at www.ICGtesting.com
Printed in the USA
LVHW080243230719
624964LV00023B/2143/P